The

ABC's

of Social Media Management

A handbook for simple, yet
effective social media
management

By Jerry Battiste

Published by Dandelion Digital Media

www.DandelionDigitalMedia.com

Know Your ABC's

Everyone wants an effective social media marketing campaign but not everyone knows how to do it.

They may be able to create a Facebook Fan Page or post content to a cool looking WordPress blog, but that hardly suffices for an effective social media marketing campaign. In fact, with a few hundred Fans or Followers you can do more harm to your company, or your product, than good.

The impact from an effective social media campaign can be measured in increased sales, increased brand recognition or increased visits and page ranking of your home page. You can create marketing messages which go viral and sweep across the global internet like a wildfire, or you can create local marketing campaigns that drive customers to your door for daily specials or weekend sales.

Effective social media campaigns have generated massive donations to charitable causes and massive sales for corporate giants and mom &

pop stores. Entire cottage industries have been developed around the ability of social media marketing to motivate buyers, for example, the numerous mobile cupcake vendors who Tweet their daily location.

Unfortunately there is no silver bullet or magic potion for developing an effective social media marketing campaign. Understanding social media, how it works and what works best, can be a tricky business. It seems everyone is offering to sell their secrets. They want to convince you they have it all figured out and if you take their three week course and shell out hundreds of dollars along the way, they will share it with you.

I have been managing blogs and social media accounts for more than a decade and I am here to tell you: There is no secret. The solution that works for your competitor might not work for you. Every business is unique and therefore requires a unique approach in how it develops an effective social media marketing campaign. You need to ask yourself what you hope to gain from your social media marketing efforts, who you want to reach and what you need them to do, then work backward from that point.

Really, it's all just a matter of common sense principles and general guidelines. Understanding the essence of social media can help you build an effective campaign. It is not so much about the tools you use, either. Many folks will tell you a Facebook Fan page is crucial to your social media campaign. Without one, they say, your campaign will go nowhere.

That is an interesting concept, because not so long ago they were saying the same things about MySpace, and before that it was Friendster. Both those companies are considered yesterday's news, Friendster is now out of business and MySpace appears poised on the brink of oblivion. Today it might be Twitter, the pre-eminent king of micro-blogging that some will point to as the quintessential social media marketing tool, but tomorrow it will likely be something else. So, pinning your social media campaign on any one specific tool is not likely to help you in the long run.

However, by understanding the concepts of an effective social media campaign, the common sense points to generating online buzz, getting visitors to your blog or website, and perhaps most importantly for some, converting those visitors into paying customers, you will be ready to handle not only the social media platforms that are in effect today, but also whatever new ones spring up next. These guidelines are simple enough to understand. This is not rocket science. It is all about understanding people, knowing what their expectations are and meeting or exceeding those expectations with your social media campaign.

Social media is hardly the end of online marketing. It is only the latest trend. But a strong trend, and the one that is working right now nonetheless. If you hope to compete in today's global economy or even just maintain market share in your community, you should understand the importance of an effective social media marketing campaign. Your customers likely understand the value of social media and use it every day. If you are not putting your business in front of that growing online audience you are missing the boat.

To help you make sense of today's social media and help you develop an effective social media marketing plan I have developed some common sense tips that anyone can understand. In "The ABC's of Social Media Management" I give you 26 tips to help make your social media efforts more effective and more likely to deliver the returns you are looking for. I kept the tips simple to understand and focused on just the basics. No tricky code to remember, no silver bullets either. Just common sense tactics that will help you develop the social media network your company needs.

Remember, it is not about the tools you employ. Effective social media management is all about the technique. Use the right technique and you can build an effective social media marketing campaign that will deliver the results you are looking for.

A

is for <u>Acknowledge</u>

Social media is perhaps the greatest communication tool to come along since the printing press. For the first time customers have a direct line of communication to the businesses they use. If they have a question, a complaint or just want to express an opinion about your product, they will likely log on to their favorite social media site and look you up there.

This means you need to be ready to **Acknowledge** them.

Nothing hurts customer relations more than to let questions go unanswered or to ignore a comment. Customers need to believe you care. Your competitors care, so you should too. If customers ask you a question online, be ready to answer those questions promptly and relevantly. If they post a comment, positive or negative be ready to respond to that too.

We all yearn to be **Acknowledged**. That's

simply a fact of life. Ignoring a customer online today is worse than ignoring them at the front counter because a disgruntled customer online can spread their displeasure to their entire network, possibly turning a viral storm of discontent your way, with just a few quick clicks of their mouse.

By the same token, you can also use social media to thank customers who have good things to say about your company, your product or your brand.

Acknowledging your customers via social media is perhaps the easiest and best way to build a good reputation online. Even if all you are doing is apologizing for poor service, it sure beats letting a dissatisfied customer fester and become more frustrated.

B

is for <u>Boasting</u>

The most effective use of social media for the purpose of marketing your company and your brand is **Boasting**. In fact, it is the best of all possible tools for letting people know just how much better your company is than your competitor.

The ability to use your network to **Boast** about your company is not only accepted on social media, it is encouraged. It is the single most common use of social media, in fact, because it is the simplest content to find.

Every employee birthday is a reason to celebrate on social media. If your company is recognized for excellence, receives an award or achieves a sales milestone, social media is a great way of getting that word out. There is no such thing as an insignificant event when it comes to **Boasting** on social media. If it is worth mentioning, even just in passing conversation, it is worth posting on your social media network. Don't miss a single opportunity to **Boast** about how great your company, your brand and your products are to the world.

There is a danger in too much **Boasting**, however. It is one thing to report something new, make an announcement or congratulate success, it is quite another thing to repeat that information over and over, or turn your social media network into a self-congratulatory soapbox. You don't need to repeatedly post links to your web site, no matter how cool it is, unless it changes regularly.

Think of the use of **Boasting** as a surgical scalpel: effective when used at the right time, in the right way, but damaging when you simply swing it around wildly. It's ok to **Boast**, just don't be boorish about it.

C

is for <u>Content</u>

When I speak to business owners about the importance of using social media to communicate with their customers and maintain a high profile online, the question I am most often asked is, "where will we get the **Content**?"

My answer is always the same: "Look in your email box."

Chances are everything you need to populate a daily blog, post status updates and Tweet on a regular basis comes to you every day. As a successful business manager you stay connected to your industry in every way possible and you expect the same of your key personnel. This industry knowledge will form the basis of your **Content** stream. Emails can be condensed and re-written; information can be abridged and condensed into bite-sized chunks for dispersing through your social media network. There is no reason to give away industry secrets, or reveal information which might prove damaging to your company or industry. Because you control the information stream you can pick and choose what information to reveal; where and when to reveal it.

You should also give serious thought to starting a daily blog.

I know, I know, you don't have time, or you don't know what to write about. Doesn't matter. The fact is, a blog is the single best way to generate new **Content** on a daily basis. And the chances are someone in your organization has the capacity to create one for you and keep it updated daily.

The problem then becomes not where to find the **Content** for your social media network, but what to do with all the **Content** you have access to. And that's a good problem to have.

D

is for <u>Damage Control</u>

I realize "**Damage Control**" is two words, but the fact is, social media is the single best tool for this all-too-common problem which faces every business at one time or another. In the digital word rumors spread at the speed of light, and the truth travels even faster. If a customer has a bad experience with a company the first thing they often do is complain about it online.

Unhappy diners post photos right from their table. These complaints are picked up and passed along and before the manager even has a chance to fix the problem, the restaurant Fan Page is inundated with negative comments.

Fortunately, as powerful a weapon as social media may be for the customer, it can also be wielded by the company. You can offer counter spin by posting immediate responses to complaints, offering discounts or simply extolling your own virtues in the community.

The worst possible way thing to do with social media is ignore. Just because your company doesn't participate in social media doesn't mean negative comments about your products or services aren't being traded about. It just means you have no idea what is being said and no opportunity to correct inaccuracies or information that is just plain untrue.

Social media is a two way street, and the road is open to everyone. If you are properly managing your social media network you will immediately know when someone has something negative to say about your brand and be able to rectify the situation or at least show other customers (and potential customers) you care about the experience they have dealing with your company.

E

is for <u>Empathy</u>

Social media is, by definition, a social endeavor. That means behaving in a way which is not only socially acceptable but also has a moral element behind it. Customers will share with you information which might not seem relevant to your business, but you still need to care.

Empathy is the key.

As human beings most of us have the capacity to share our feelings with others and respond to the feelings which are shared with us. This is how we build relationships; true lasting relationships that eventually benefit us, either as a result of business opportunities or simply through strong enduring friendships.

Empathy is what kept people coming to their corner grocer or local baker even as big chain shopping centers opened up around the country. It is what drives us to find a plumber, electrician or automobile mechanic we trust. Yes, we want quality work, but we also want someone we can build a relationship with. Showing Empathy is easy when you use social media. Just interact via your network. Show them that you have **Empathy**.

If a customer cares enough to share information with you take that as a sign they think you are worthy of their trust. Don't be afraid to comment on photos or posts even when they do not seem relevant to your business or your brand.

Empathy is a powerful tool. When you show you care about your customers they will reciprocate. Your caring will enhance your relationship with them. Their caring will likely translate into increased revenue.

F

is for <u>Free</u>

Social media is a great way to get information out about special offers. And the best offers are those which offer customers something for **Free**. **Free** offers are traded around the social media landscape like currency. They are "gifted" to users by their friends and co-workers and are among the most commonly re-posted items on the Internet. This has led to a proliferation of daily coupon sites which see the best results from their "buy one get one **Free**" deals.

If you want to get the most bang for your social media buck, come up with some **Free** or highly discounted deals and promote these through your social media network.

This is the moment when many of my clients just stare at me blankly and ask, "Like what?" Or, I have the clients who want to give away a **Free** iPad every week or a gold coin to the lucky 1000th Fan on their Facebook page.

Think smaller, folks.

The fact is, people like getting something for nothing. It doesn't matter much what that thing is, just that it's **Free**. It's a compulsion for many of us, to seek out and claim as many **Free** things as we possibly can. This is the same urge which drives every kid to dump out the entire box of cereal in order to get to the cheap plastic toy buried inside, and cry like babies if their older sibling got to it first.

If you don't have a business that lends itself to simple and inexpensive giveaways, consider some easy alternatives like stickers, posters, pencils or anything with your logo printed on it. In the end, it won't matter as much what sort of things you give away, but the frequency with which you give them away. Remember, **Free** is good.

G

is for <u>Gateway</u>

As great as it may be, your social media network is still just a **Gateway** for your web site. Ultimately what you want is to drive visitors (Followers, Fans, whatever) to the place where you can close the deal. While it is helpful to have a large social media network what you really want are paying customers. It is imperative you have a way to turn those social media users into revenue.

So when you begin designing your social media network be certain you plan with the end in mind. Have links and similarly simple ways for customers to get from your social media site to your web site, or even better, use the social media sites themselves to arrange contact; schedule appointments or order products. Opt-in email lists, links and free offers for web visitors are just a few of the tools that can help re-direct social media users to your point-of-sale.

Well designed landing pages and content

funnels play a crucial role in turning visitors into clients or customers, so be certain you have done your home work and have these systems in place before you start driving your social media network in that direction.

Your social media network is your **Gateway** to what you really have to offer. But like every **Gateway** it needs to look appealing and attractive in order to bring people in.

You should also design your social media network so there is continuity and symmetry between it and your web site. People don't want to feel as if they have changed boats mid-stream, so watch the color schemes as well. The transition from your social network your website should be perfectly seamless.

H

is for <u>Habit</u>

Using social media must become a **Habit**. If you post something new only once a week or heaven forbid, once per month, your network will not grow. The same can be said for a lack of response to comments or questions posted within your social media network. Your network must be carefully monitored daily. Customers left without answers are like customers left waiting at the front counter for someone to take their order.

Most companies recognize this and hire social media professionals to handle the day-to-day work of monitoring and maintaining their social media network. If you are dealing with limited resources then consider starting with a smaller social network and spreading the task around to multiple people in your organization.

But don't bite off more than you can chew. If you are going to create a social media network you have to manage it properly. Failure to do so can hurt your company more than having no social media network at all.

Turning a mundane task into a Habit has more to do with the psychology of the person assigned to the task than it does with the task itself, so make certain you aren't asking anyone to completely alter their daily routine. Or if you are, make certain they understand the importance of what they are doing.

You will also need to monitor your social media network yourself, at least initially, or assign the job of monitoring it to someone separate from the person who is managing it. You need a system of checks and balances to be certain your network is being regularly updated in the manner you need it to be. This is good practice for you, as well as your social media manager.

Learn how to make managing your social media network a **Habit**, then train your employees to do the same.

I

is for <u>Immediate</u>

Social media is not a "when I get around to it" institution. The whole idea of social media is to let people know what you are doing right now. That requires a sense of urgency; an ability to react as soon as a conversation starts or a request for information has been made.

Unfortunately, when it comes to social media there is no automation available to help make this happen for you. In fact, automating your social media network would negate the benefits of building a social network. After all, social media marketing is relationship marketing and nobody wants to have a relationship with an automaton.

You can use a tool such as Tweetadder to monitor Twitter for specific key words and phrases and Follow or UnFollow other users based on these parameters, but this is only effective for Twitter. The social web is much, much bigger than Twitter.

The only solution you have available is to

properly train the people you have managing your network for you. Even if you have a professional social media management team monitoring and managing your social media network it still wouldn't hurt for you to check in every now and then and make certain your customers, and potential customers, are being responded to in a manner which is proper, efficient and above all else, **Immediate**.

This goes back to making a Habit of using social media. The more you can integrate social media into your existing work system, the easier it will be to manage and the more **Immediate** your response time will become.

Remember, nobody likes to be kept waiting and when it comes to social media, the sooner the better.

J

is for <u>Jargon</u>

Interacting on social media does not need to be difficult. In fact, it is one of the easiest possible ways to promote your brand and business, provided you know how to talk to people and can avoid boring them to death with industry **Jargon**.

This goes back to the whole, social media marketing is relationship marketing concept I mentioned earlier.

Have you ever found yourself in conversation with someone who continuously uses their industry **Jargon** in the conversation? You probably found yourself constantly asking, "what does that mean?" letting your mind drift or finding the nearest exit to escape the conversation.

This is what will happen on social media if you constantly resort to industry-speak.

Perhaps your company makes widgets; the finest widgets in the world. People who follow you may want to know about the process for making widgets, but they need you to explain it to them in the simplest possible terms. You are the widget expert. You know all the terminology. Your customers likely do not.

Yes, you certainly can attract a number of industry professionals to your social media network, and these people might want to talk shop with you every now and then. But in all likelihood the customers you are looking to attract are novices when it comes to widget making. Besides, anyone who wants intricate details about widget making can find other ways aside from your social media network to get the answers they need.

Your social media network is about being sociable. You wouldn't go to a Christmas party and start talking shop, so don't do it on your social media network.

K

is for <u>Knowledge</u>

Knowledge is the currency of the Internet, particularly social media. What you **Know** is what people want to hear about. Saying this, I want to remind you about the need to avoid "Jargon" and suggest you find ways to present what you **Know** in easily digestible chunks.

People want to learn from you, but they don't want to be lectured, or talked down to. You would be surprised at how far your **Knowledge** of plumbing, electrical work, automobiles, the stock market, hair styling, films, fashion, tanning or food can get you when it comes to expanding your social media network. Along the way you are marketing your business by demonstrating your expertise in your particular field.

No need to give away trade secrets or reveal everything you **Know** in a single day and one ultra-lengthy blog post. Space it out. Remember, juicy bite-sized pieces are preferable to choking your reader to death with a bunch of dry facts.

There is a line between using your **Knowledge** to expand the reach of your brand and giving it all away for free. Social media can help you accomplish one without resorting to the other.

I like to say that **Knowledge** is the true currency of the Internet. What you know has value. Used properly it can be effectively used to increase your brand awareness and drive people to your door (or website.)

If you have **Knowledge**, and I am sure you do if you have a business or brand to market, that **Knowledge** is power in the social media world. Use it wisely.

L

is for <u>Learn</u>

You might be interested in hiring a professional social media manager to handle your social media marketing or you might want to do it yourself. Either way, I recommend you **Learn** at least the basics about social media before you begin.

In fact, **Learning** more than the basics is even better.

Personally, I don't mind if a client comes to me with no knowledge of social media and asks me to set-up their network. I do mind if they have no clear understanding of how social media marketing works and begin expecting the impossible.

There are a host of social media tools available for you to use to market your brand, your products or your business. It is not important for you to **Learn** everything there is to know about all of them. But you should try to keep up with the changes that are constantly occurring in the industry; know who the major players are and what role they can assume in your social media marketing plan.

Let me repeat, I am not here to tell you what tools to use; the tools change all the time. What you need to **Learn** are what the latest tools are, how they work and whether or not they could work for you.

The way you know which tools will work best for your marketing plan is to have a good grasp of the audience you want to reach, and what you expect them to do. Maybe you need to reach young urban professionals interested in reducing their carbon footprint or investing for their futures; or homeowners who want to cut their energy bills or make home improvements.

Each of these groups is best reached in a specific way using a specific type of social media. The tools to reach them will change before you finish reading this book, but they won't.

M

is for <u>Measure</u>

As I write these words no one yet has found an effective way to **Measure** the results of social media marketing across all fields. Some people will tell you to look at certain analytics, check your influence score or track your visitors, but they still won't be able to tell you the true impact of your social media marketing efforts.

That's where I suggest you use a little common sense.

You need to **Measure** the impact of your social media marketing efforts so you know what works and what doesn't. This will help you focus in on the tools that do the most good for your business and produce the best results. The way to do this is to use the system to produce **Measurable** results.

For instance, you can ask your social network visitors to opt-in to a company newsletter, respond to a few questions or even visit your brick and mortar store for a free offer. These suggestions will produce hard, **Measurable** results.

What good does it do your company to have 50,000 social media friends if you can't get any of them to complete a survey? Or, if you post a store wide sale on your status update page and no one shows up, how much good is that social media site doing for your bottom line?

You can hire an analytics firm to produce reams of data about the traffic to various portions of your network, but if you really want to know what the return on your investment is, produce something **Measurable** and a lot more meaningful.

The fact is, although social media is not a costly endeavor, it does take time. And as every business person knows, time is money. So make the best use of your time by focusing on the portions of your social media network which produce **Measurable** results.

N

is for <u>Network</u>

Remember, what you are building is a social media **Network** to help you market your business. The larger your social media **Network** is, the farther your message will travel and the more effective it will be.

This **Network** will likely be comprised of at least a few different social media sites, depending on the demographic profile of the people you want to reach. In this way, the **Network** itself becomes the most valuable social media marketing tool. No single piece of the **Network** is more important than any other, for the **Network** functions together.

Blogs link to websites; websites promote social media profiles, which in turn promote the web site and blogs. Photos are posted and videos, which also refer visitors back to your web site or blog, which simply circle people back around to your social media again.

As I have said before, it doesn't matter which

blog platform or social networks you use. Pick the ones which work best for your system and reach the demographic you are aiming for. Do some research. Find out which system has the simplest interface, the broadest reach and the best chance of delivering the results you are looking. You will likely need to try a few of them before you find the ones which work best for you, but that's all part of the Learning process.

I could name a few tools, but the fact is those tools will eventually become outdated, replaced by new, more innovative tools that deliver a completely new social media experience. In this way, the tools don't matter.

The **Network** is the only tool that matters. The **Network** has the value. Build the **Network** as big and grand or simple and small as you like, so long as it meets your needs and serves you ultimate purpose. And as long as it is manageable.

O

is for <u>Outsourcing</u>

If your internal resources are stretched to the limit, don't be afraid to **Outsource** your social media marketing workload. This can be as simple as hiring a blogger to produce content, or a social media manager to set-up and manage your social media network.

Everything from website design to web content to traffic analytics can be done on an as-needed basis. No need to break the bank trying to create a social media marketing network. With **Outsourcing**, you make arrangements that fit your budget.

Also, by **Outsourcing** your social media management you stand a better chance of creating a more manageable social media marketing network. You will be able to scrutinize each piece as it comes together, instead of jumping in with both feet, eyes closed, fingers pinching your nose shut.

Outsourcing has become a dirty word,

representing a company which prefers the cheapest alternative, or is willing to settle for reduced quality at the expense of their customers.

But **Outsourcing** can be a effective tool for making your company more productive and creating a better experience for your customers and clients. There is no logic in expecting your employees to build a social media network while they continue to handle their day-to-day responsibilities. If you are the only employee in your company you don't have time to handle social media management and keep up with everything else you need to do.

When it comes to effective social media management, and resources are limited, **Outsourcing** makes a whole lot more sense.

P

is for <u>Patience</u>

Once you start down the path of creating your social media marketing network be ready to do some serious waiting. Rome was not built in a day and neither shall your network. It will take time and **Patience** to train your existing customers to find your company online. Once they begin finding you online it will take time for them to spread the news around to their friends.

I like to tell my clients that social media management is a marathon, not a sprint. Don't expect to build your network overnight.

Unless you are giving away gold bullion, or you are a world famous celebrity, it is going to take you months to build a respectable network and start seeing some serious returns for your social media marketing efforts.

Saying this, I know some social media marketing professionals will tell you they can get you thousands of Followers and Friends in days, if not hours. This is likely true. But what you want are customers, people who are interested in buying your products, visiting your stores or supporting your brand. Followers and Friends can help you get the word out about your company, but they won't necessarily bring in the revenue you are looking for.

In order to build a truly effective social media network you need a strong foundation, built on trust. Trust does not come easily and only time can deliver a trusting relationship. People like to visit stores, companies and individuals whom they can trust to deliver exactly what they need. This trust came only with time.

So be **Patient**. Social media is not a numbers game. Give your network time to grow and expand and you will be rewarded with real results that make a difference to your bottom line.

Q
is for <u>Quality</u>

Above all else, your social media network must produce quality information; integrity is of the utmost importance.

I cannot emphasize this enough.

Do not be tempted by those who promise to "buy" you Followers. Do not be tempted by those who promise to "automate" your social media postings.

Quality has value in the brick and mortar world and it has value online. In fact, the value of **Quality** online is enhanced simply because there is less of it on the Internet than many people would care to admit.

By producing a stream of **Quality** information on your social media network you are producing content which will entice people to follow what you say. Visitors will be attracted to your social media network because of **Quality** content, and they will be more likely to pass along that content because it can be relied upon to be accurate, interesting and decidedly "spam free."

If you want your information passed around the Internet, don't flood your social media network with an abundance of pointless, self-aggrandizing press releases. These will not entice potential clients or lead to increased revenue. In fact, too much poor-quality information and you could have the reverse effect and begin to drive people away from your company.

Instead provide a the same level of **Quality** social engagement as the product or service you represent and it will provide similar benefits in the long run. It will also help you build trust with the people in your network which will ultimately convert than to paying customers.

Quality. Don't forget I said that.

R
is for <u>Relevant</u>

If your company business is plumbing then I recommend that your social media network reflect that. Dispense plumbing tips, news and information about the latest plumbing trends; designer fixtures or new technology; things that are **Relevant** to your trade. This will help lend credence to the idea that you are an expert in your field.

If you begin posting information about cookie recipes or reality television reviews, visitors may get confused about what you do. Off-topic information certainly will not help you win new customers, and might potentially cost you some customers who come looking for knowledge but find useless commentary instead.

So too should your social media network names reflect the essence of your business. Make certain you choose a **Relevant** blog title; figure your industry prominently in your web site design and use your social media network to connect with others in your industry so you are part of the larger industry network.

That does not mean you cannot go off topic every now and then to keep your network interesting. There is nothing wrong with expressing an opinion about something outside your usual purview. How often you do this depends a great deal on how often your social network requires it and what conversations you might step into.

If conversations on your network abound about the latest round of Oscar nominations, don't be afraid to chime in. Someone in your company has likely been to the movies, most people have at one time or another, and having an opinion about a favorite movie or actor is a socially acceptable thing to do. On the other hand if your business is not directly involved with politics or religion, avoid those conversations at all costs.

S

is for <u>Spam</u>

Back at letter "Q" when I talked about the importance of Quality when it came to the information you put out through your social media network, I mentioned that dreaded of all Internet terms, "**Spam.**"

Now I am mentioning it again. For our purposes, "**Spam**" refers to Internet junk mail, not the delicious canned meat product.

"**Spam**" is not just annoying, it is also illegal in some instances and will get your account shut down on sites like Facebook and Twitter. Nobody likes "**Spam**". It clogs up the Internet and does practically no good at all. As a marketing tool you would be better off dropping leaflets out of an airplane over a city which doesn't speak your language than you would be using "**Spam**" to get your message across.

It is important you understand exactly what is meant by "**Spam**" so you will recognize it before you send it. In some cases **"Spam"** is not so much about the message as it is about the way the message is spread.

Forcing a message on someone, like a web site which plays an annoying commercial every time someone visits, or a link which promises one thing, but delivers a commercial message first, these are considered by many people to be **"Spam"** techniques. Creating a data base of email addresses and sending out mass self-promoting emails without first being asked by the recipients for this information, is another form of **"Spam."**

When it comes to social media, any attempts at **"Spamming"** your Friends or Followers may not only get your account shut down, but may also lead to people spreading the word that your company uses unscrupulous marketing tactics. As any good business-person knows, bad word-of-mouth advertising can hurt your reputation for months, possibly years, costing your company revenue.

T

is for <u>Timely</u>

Be aware that social media moves at the speed of right now.

Posting to your blog once a month, or even once a week, simply will not work. Your blog needs to be updated every day. Your social media network itself should be monitored at about every hour, with a focus on participating in conversations which are happening in real-time.

Even your web page should be renewed and revamped at least once per year. Some elements of your web page should have current information on them every day, so returning visitors find something new.

If the information on your web page never changes there is little reason for anyone to return, right?

This type of time commitment leads some companies to forego using social media. They prefer the days when a static web page was enough to get the job done. Hopefully, that is the way your competitor is thinking because it will put them right out of business, or at least keep their company from growing and capturing any more market share.

Timeliness is also crucial when it comes to responding to comments posted to your company through its social network. Leaving questions or concerns unanswered is a recipe for public relations disaster.

When you are updating your social media network you need to be **Relevant** and **Timely**. Participate in conversations that are happening right now and comment on events which are as current as possible. In this way your social media network will seem like a living growing part of your company instead of something you are just putting on for show.

U

is for <u>United</u>

Your social media marketing effort is all about the theory of there being strength in numbers. By **Uniting** a multitude of social media tools you create a communications network which is greater than the sum of its parts.

The idea behind effective social media management is to leverage your various network users to help promote your company or your brand. You do this by sending messages out and hoping they will be picked up and passed along.

In order to make the best use of your social media network it is important that you present a **United** front. Every tool in your social media arsenal should be working in conjunction with every other tool; self-promoting, sharing and re-directing like a chain of dominoes that lead inexorably to a glorious finish.

The message you want to pass through your social media network needs to be crafted specifically for each of your various social media properties. Your message might begin as a blog post, then be shortened and sent out on Twitter with a link back to your blog. On Facebook you can offer a longer message with more detail and also include a link back to your original blog.

The same goes for every other social media site you have, but avoid the temptation of simply repeating the same message over and over again. Tailor the message to fit each particular aspect of your social media network, make it unique, but stay on the same message.

With all the pieces of your social media network working together you are in a much better position to spread your message the way you intend and in a way which will bring you the results you are looking for.

Remember, your social media network should be a **United** front. Making it so is all about proper management.

V

is for <u>Video</u>

You may not realize it, but YouTube is consistently rated as one of the Top 10 most popular search engines on the Internet.

I know I said I wasn't going to focus on the tools, but **Video** is the fastest growing new media on the Internet, bar none, and for now, YouTube has cornered the market on **Video** and nobody is anywhere close to catching up to them.

Web surfers often go to YouTube when they have a question because they know it is very likely someone else has had a similar problem and made a **Video** how-to showing others what the solution is.

Knowing this, what are you waiting for? Using the **Knowledge** you already possess your company should have a YouTube channel and use it to offer your own how-to **Videos**.

Maybe you can demonstrate how to install a ceiling fan (if you specialize in electrical work) or talk about investing in foreign markets (if you are financial traders.) Whatever your industry you have the potential to start shooting instructional **Videos** right away.

These don't have to be slick, professionally produced **Videos**. Get yourself a $100 digital video camera, line up your best looking, in-house expert, and shoot a 90 second **Video** on a topic specific to your brand. Or, use a laptop with a built-in web cam and shoot direct. They also make software to record what is happening on your desktop while you record the audio with the built-in microphone.

Whatever type of **video** you want to shoot, there are inexpensive tools to help you get it done. If you are unsure what to put in your **video**, try doing a search for **videos** within your area of expertise.

Imitation is the sincerest form of flattery after all.

W

is for <u>Welcoming</u>

With your new social media network in play you will likely encounter a number of new friends, fans, partners, employees, customers, clients and potential all-of-the-above.

Be ready for them. Be advised they might not all have positive things to say. But above all else, be **Welcoming**.

Your social media network should be open to anyone and everyone who wants to visit. Every new visitor is a potential partner in the network you want to build or the one you have already established. Welcome them and make them feel **Welcome**.

Encourage conversations and solicit feedback. Engage them and see what they have to say about your brand, your company and what your future plans might mean for them. Look to them for advice and don't be afraid to take a little criticism from them every now and then.

Just like an unwanted party guest, if they get out of hand you can always have them escorted out; banned from the network. But only use this as a last resort. Remember, everything you do online is open to public scrutiny. If you start banning everyone who has something negative to say about your company, brand or product, it will look as if there is merit in what they say and that you have something to hide.

So throw the doors to your social media network open wide, but be ready for anyone to walk in off the street. Proper maintenance and management of your social media network will keep everyone in line and make certain decorum is maintained, and you'll have a network known for its honesty and **Welcoming** nature which will go a long way toward building **Trust**.

X

is for <u>Xylograph</u>

Do you know what a **Xylograph** is? If you do, go get yourself a cookie right now!

A **Xylograph** is a wood engraving, or, when you take a wood engraving and make an impression with it, the image is called a **Xylograph**. Once upon a time a **Xylograph** was the coolest, most technologically advanced way to communicate information. No color, no 3D images, no moving pictures (unless you shuffled a handful of them around like a deck of cards) just simple black and white prints.

Despite its simplicity, there is little doubt the **Xylograph** was at least partially responsible for urging people to create new and better ways to tell stories, share information and communicate. As those new things came along, namely paper, the printing press, telecommunications and whatnot, the **Xylograph** fell out favor.

The same thing will happen to the social

media sites which are much in favor today. They will fade away and be replaced by something new, more advanced or at least more popular.

This won't affect you, however, because you remember the **Xylograph** and you know that it isn't the instrument you use to communicate that is important, it's the message you are communicating that matters most. So your social media network might change sites from time to time, but the mission, the urgency of getting your message out to the widest possible audience, will remain the same. No matter what tools you use to make that happen.

That's why I have been telling you not to focus so much on the tools. The tools will change, give way to new and better tools. But the lessons you learn about how best to use the tools you have now will help you better use the tools that are coming tomorrow.

Y

is for <u>Yearbook</u>

One of the most unrecognized advantages of having a social media network is the ability to establish a **Yearbook** of events pertaining to your business. From a marketing stand point this information, comprised of past accolades, achievements and awards, is invaluable.

With your social media network you can post photos from events like the office Christmas party (minus the embarrassing moments); finished projects, new products, new equipment and employees hard at work.

Every day your company is producing reams of memorable information.

With a social media network you can not only store this information where it is easily retrievable, but also share it with people around the world and use it to further promote your brand.

When you offer people an inside glimpse of your business they feel as if they are getting something special, like a behind-the-scenes guided tour. This is the type of information that will keep them coming back for more, while providing your company a tool for recording your day-to-day activities.

Sharing information like this is also a great way to build relationships with the people in your social media network. Relationships are what bind the best networks together. People share information because they think it is interesting or relevant for their own personal networks, and sometimes they share information just to do someone else a favor.

The strength of the relationships you have with the people in your network will determine how likely they are to share your information. And you strengthen those relationships by sharing information about your company; putting a face on your business and making it personal.

Z

is for <u>Zoo</u>

Let's be honest: The Internet is a **Zoo**.

There are all manner of people doing all manner of things online any time of the day or night.

As a business person, or a marketer interested in using social media for your clients, you want to keep the insanity of the Internet at a safe distance from your secure environment. This is prudent and possible, to a degree, but the fact is every now and then something is bound to happen within your seemingly safe and secure social media environment that you would prefer had not. Someone will post an off-color comment, or say something unflattering and untrue about your brand or your product.

The best advice I can give you is to be as prepared as possible, but expect the worst. Having someone specific manage your social media is a start, but remember, given the 24/7 nature of the

Internet, something is bound to happen. When it does, don't panic. There are systems in place to filter language, prevent spammy links and block specific users for bad behavior. Learn what they are and be ready to use them. It's not a question of if it will happen, but when it will happen, so get used to it.

There is no point losing sleep over what someone might post to your network. Have your management systems in place to handle these inevitabilities and let the system take care of itself. That's what it's there for.

About The Author

Jerry Battiste is a professional social media manager, blogger and freelance writer. He is the co-founder of Dandelion Digital Media which specializes in delivering effective social media marketing for small-medium sized businesses.

He was a successful daily print news reporter and photographer for more than a decade and was among the first in the print news industry to integrate social media into his daily news reporting, utilizing Twitter, Facebook and YouTube to report the news and provide more in-depth coverage for his readers.

Jerry Battiste is currently the author of two books: "The ABC's of Social Media Management" and a collection of short fiction called "8 Lucky."

He lives in Muncie, Indiana where he is busily working on yet another useful digital media handbook and more short fiction. You can visit his website for more information, Friend him on Facebook, Follow him on Twitter or add him to your Circles on Google+.